Fashion
Sketches

Coloring Book

COLOR TEST PAGE

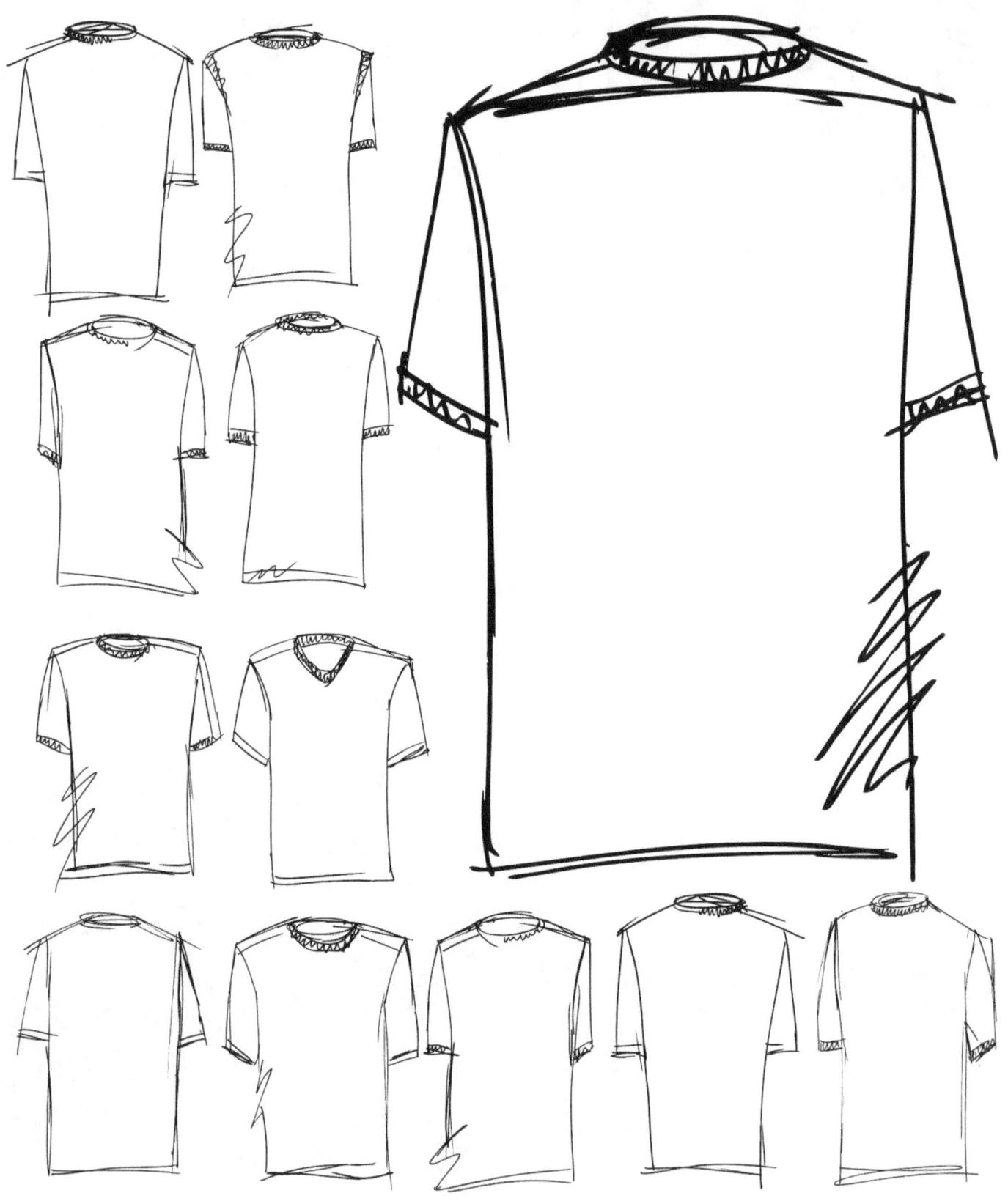

COLOR TEST PAGE

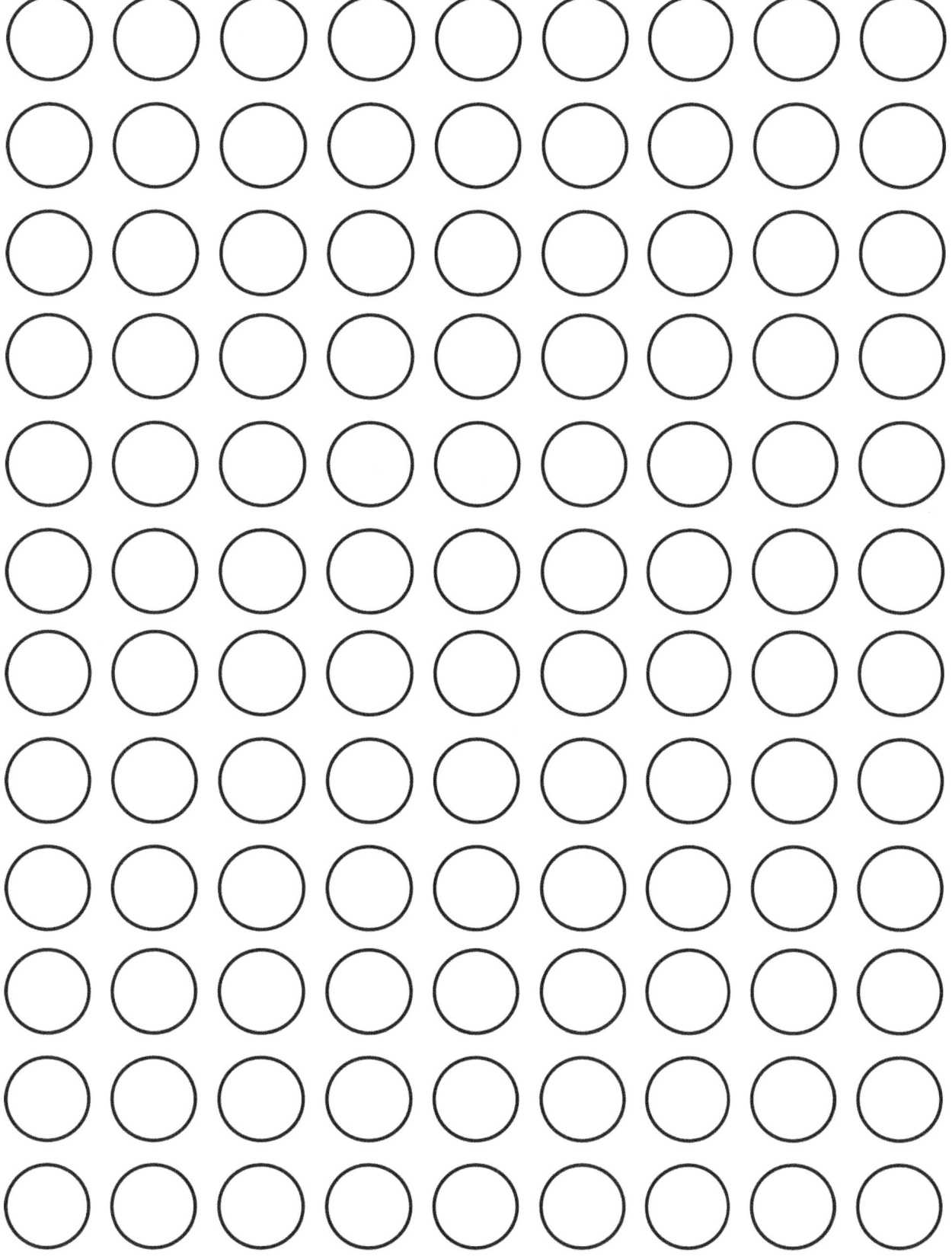

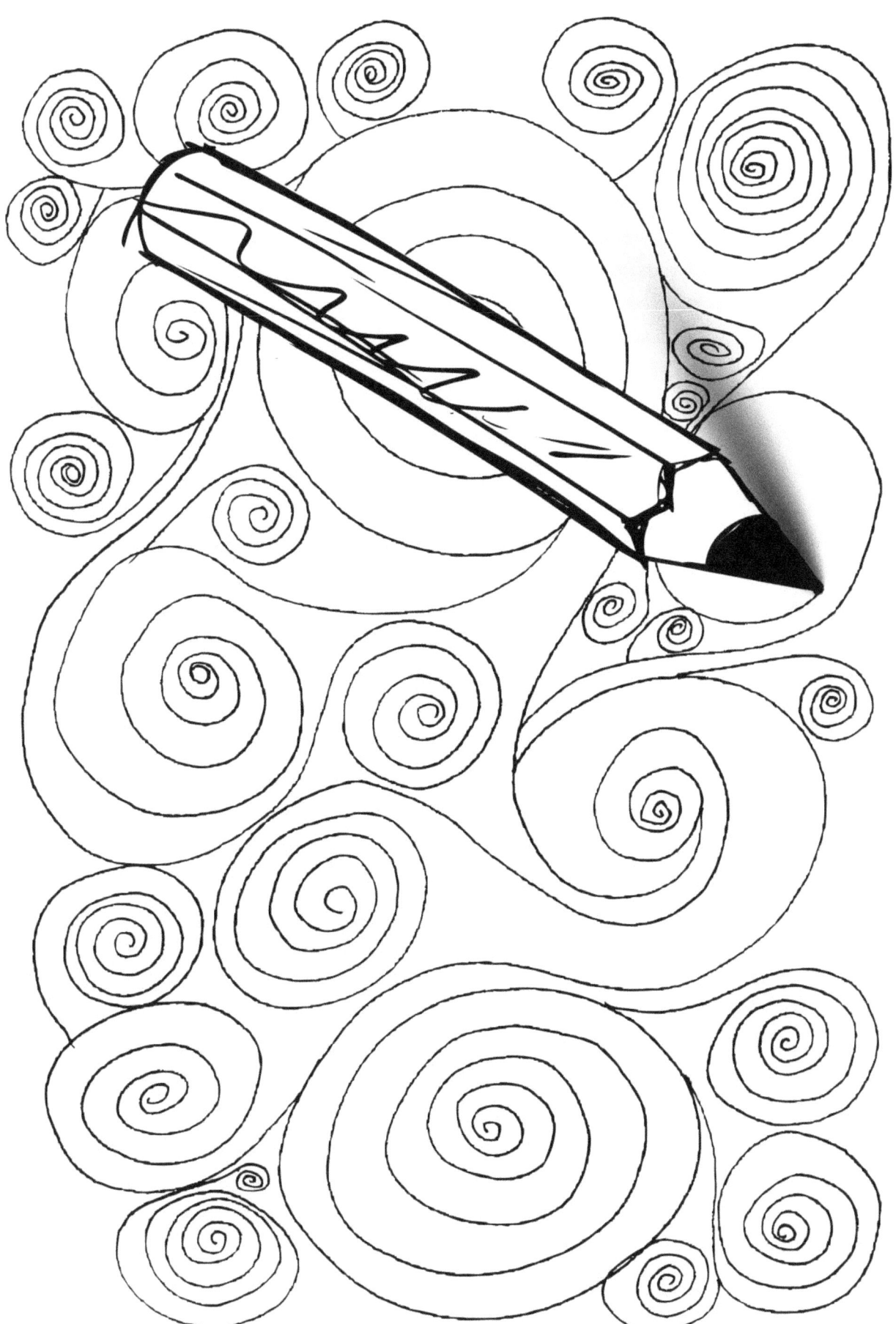

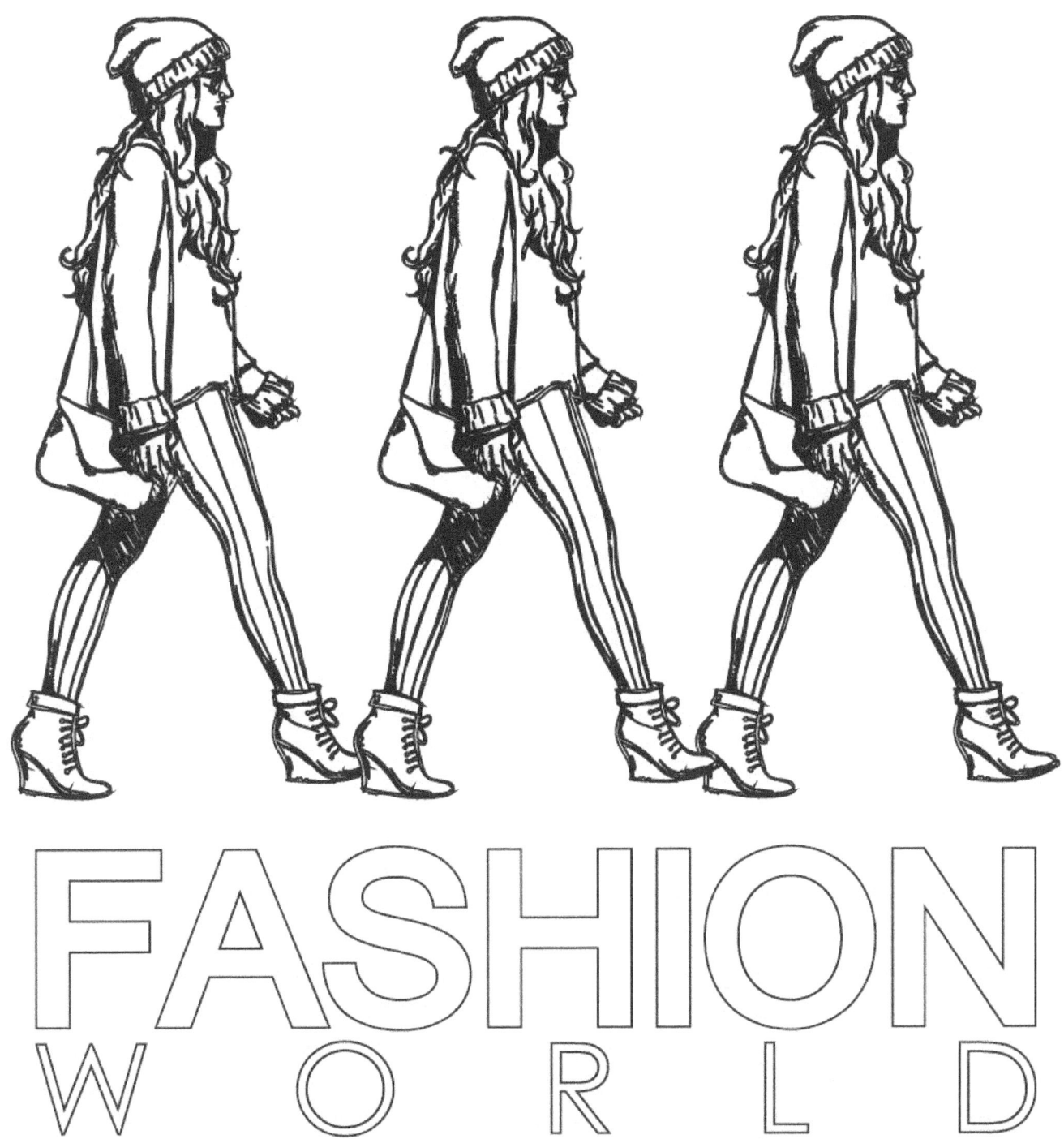

FASHION
WORLD

Milano New York Paris Rome London Los Angeles Hong Kong
Sao Paulo Sydney Las Vegas Dubai Tokyo Miami Barcelona Shanghai
Mumbai New Delhi Rio de Janeiro Berlin Singapore Madrid Moscow
Santiago Melbourne Stockholm Bangkok Krakow Prague Mexico City

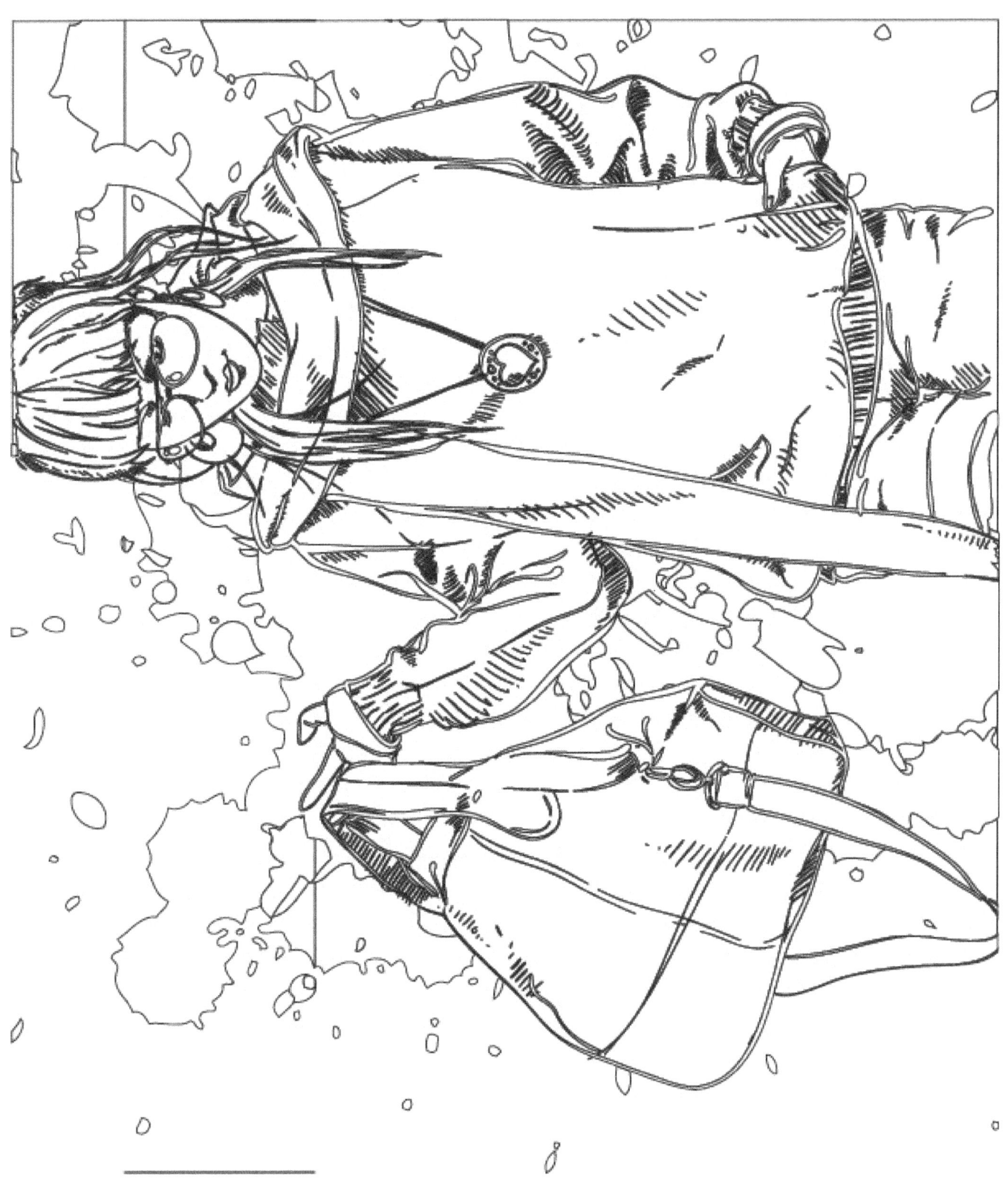

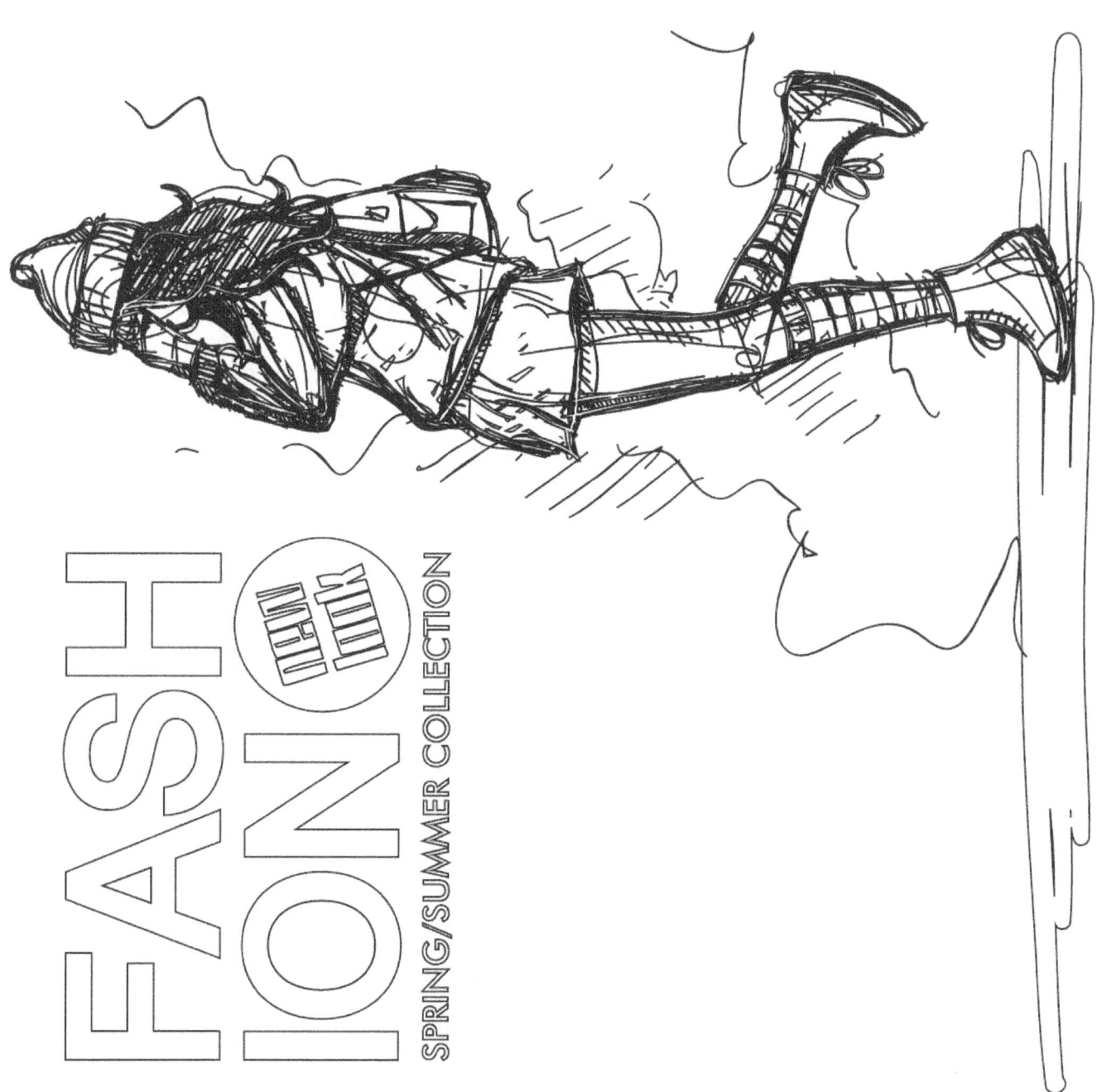

FASH
ION

SPRING/SUMMER COLLECTION

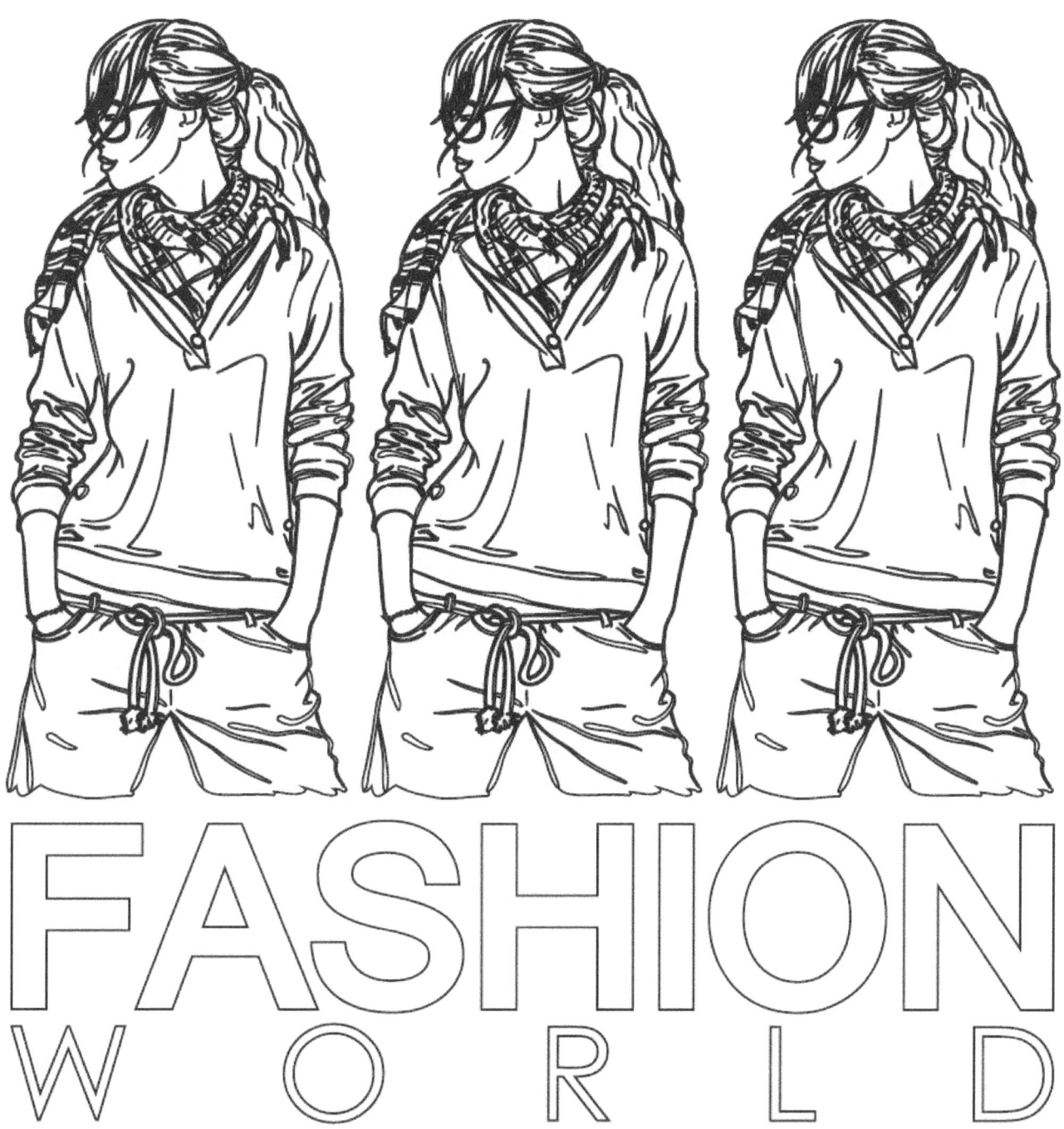

FASHION
WORLD

Milano New York Paris Rome London Los Angeles Hong Kong
Sao Paulo Sydney Las Vegas Dubai Tokyo Miami Barcelona Shanghai
Mumbai New Delhi Rio de Janeiro Berlin Singapore Madrid Moscow
Santiago Melbourne Stockholm Bangkok Krakow Prague Mexico City

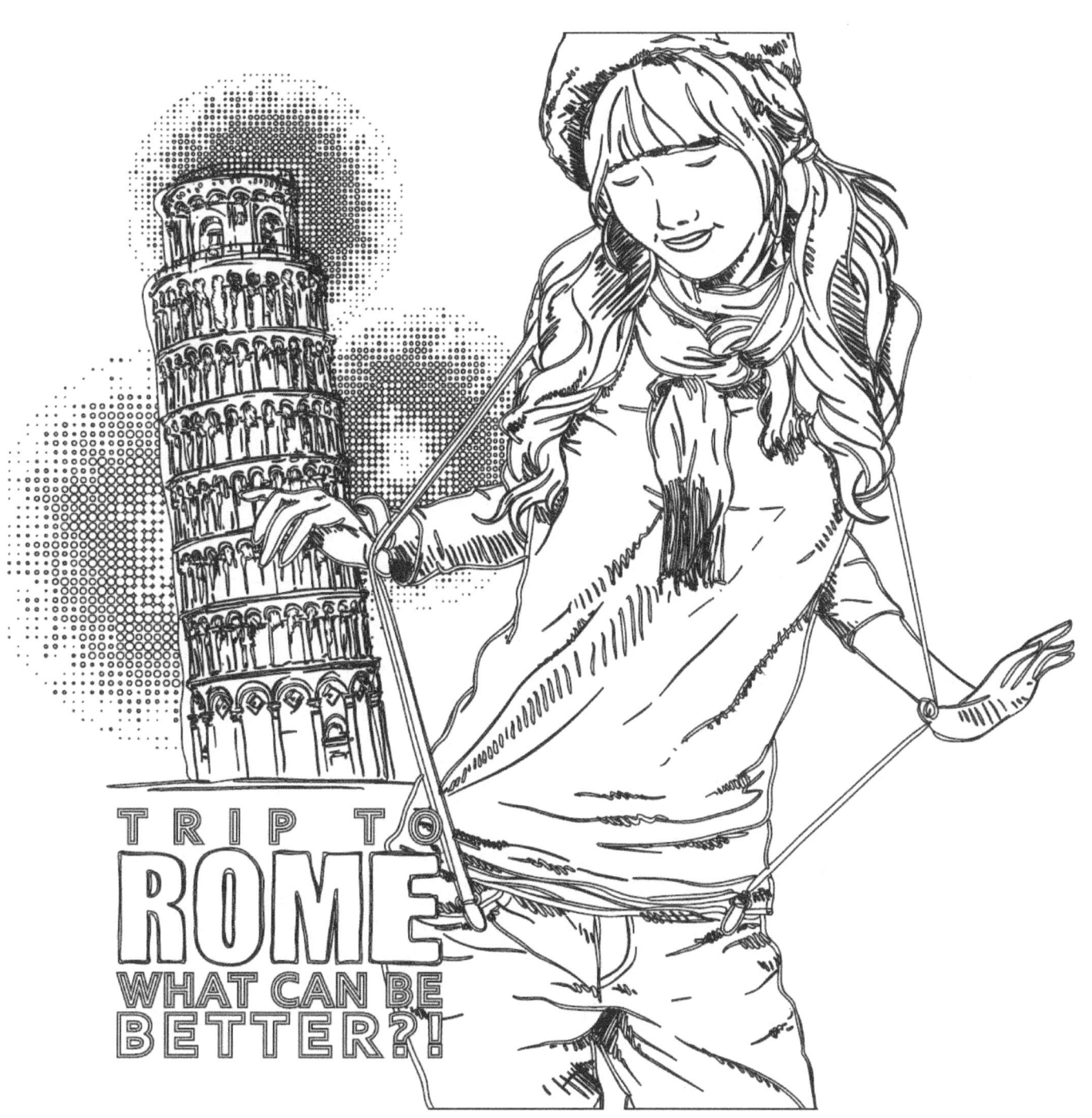

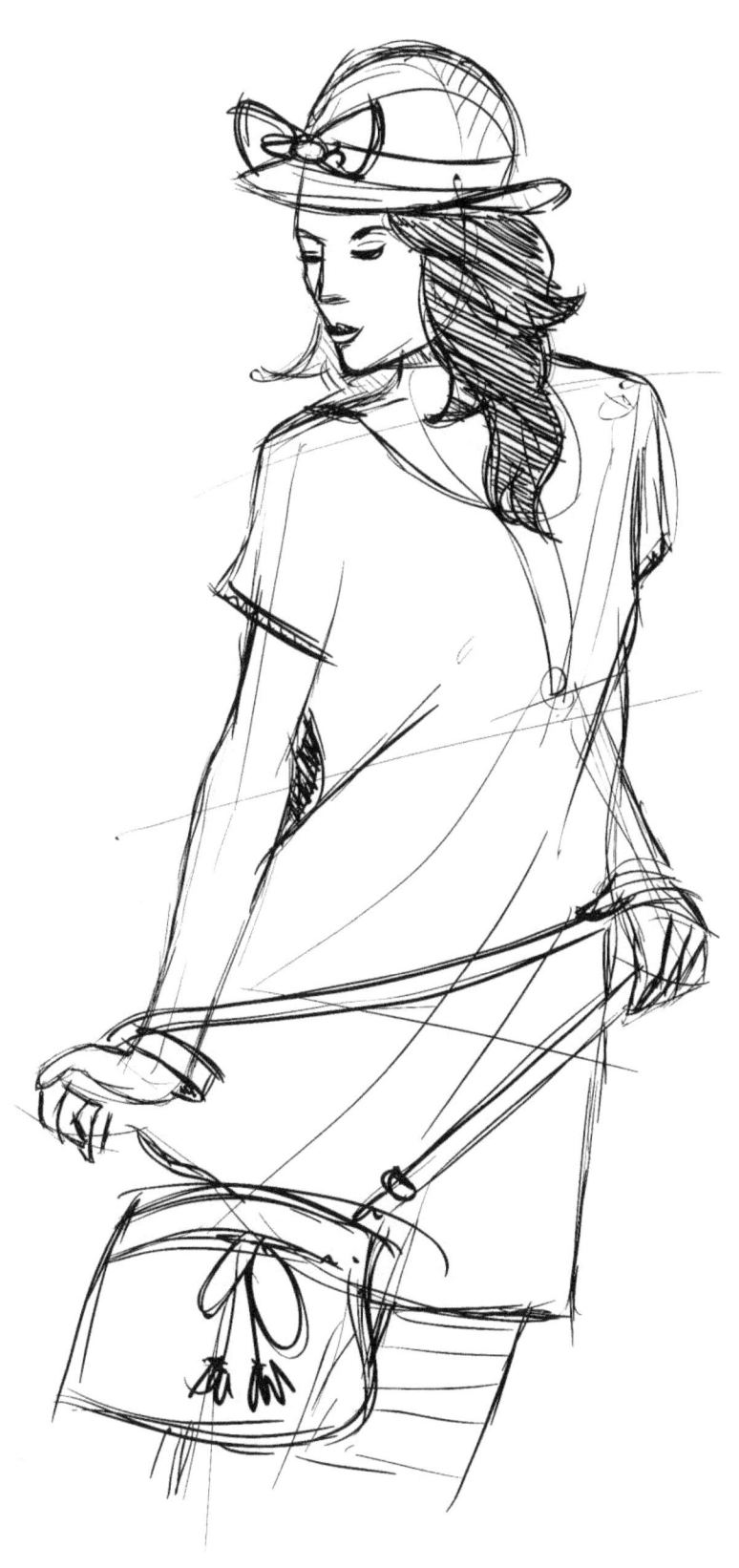

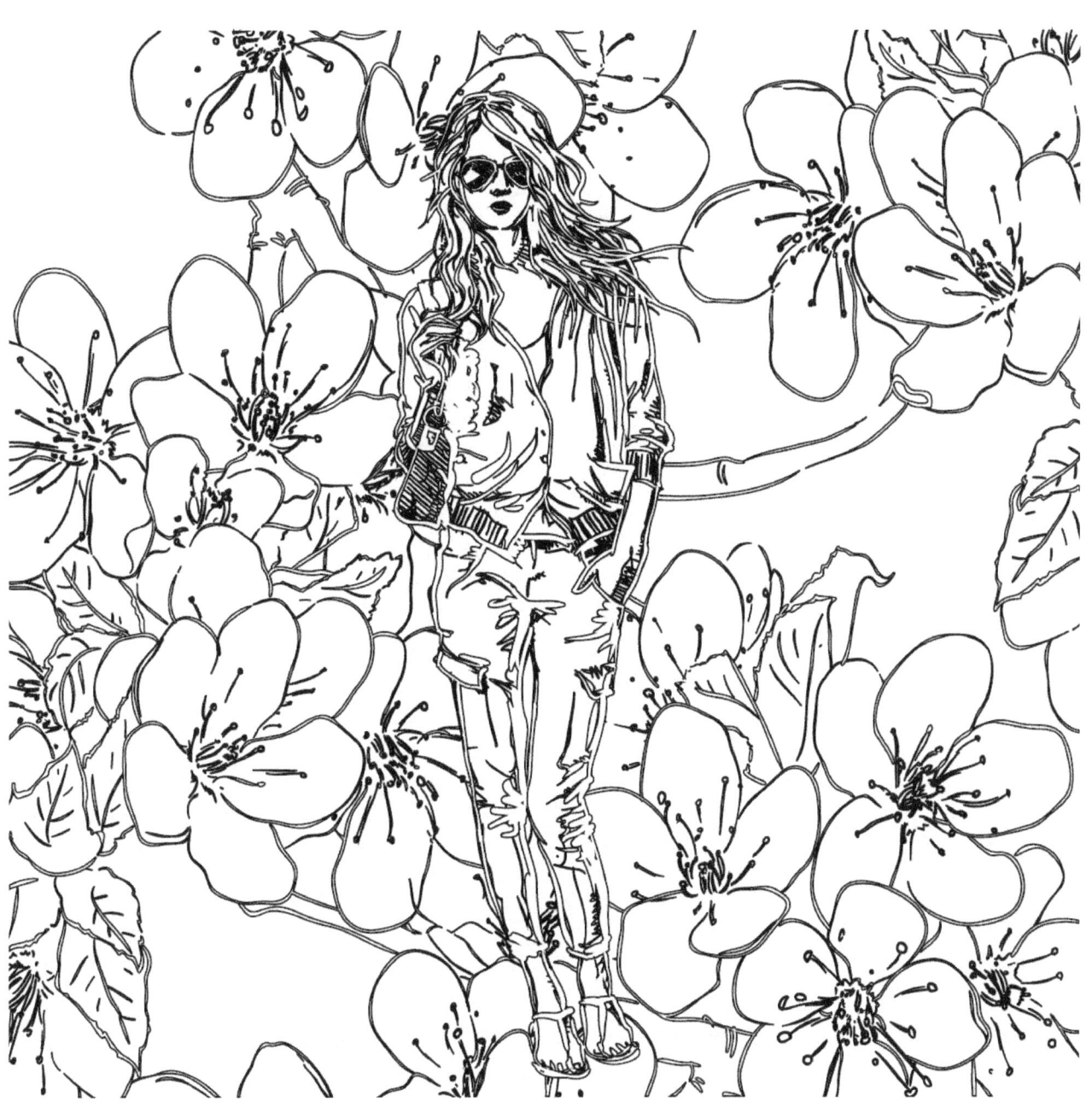

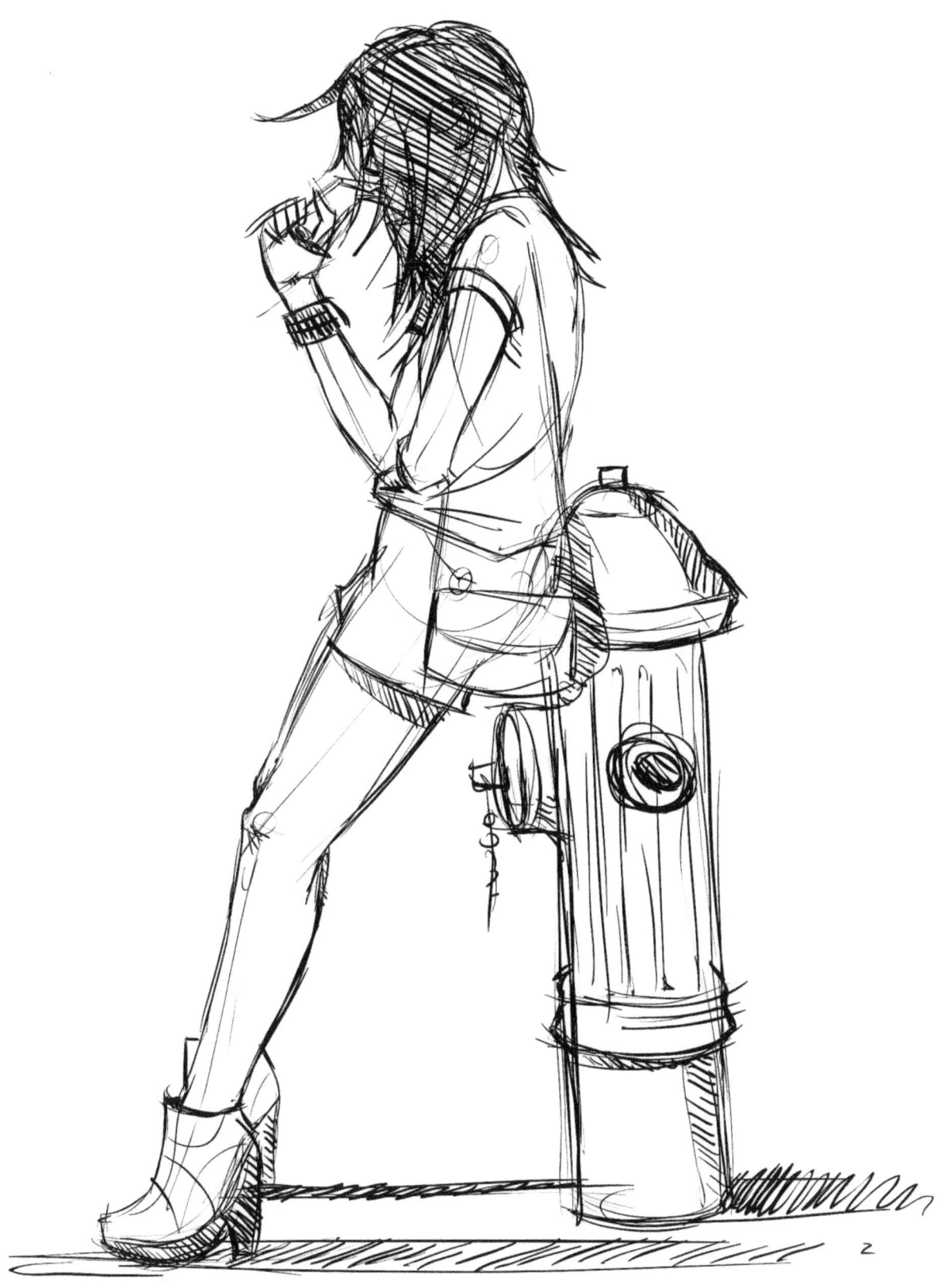

2

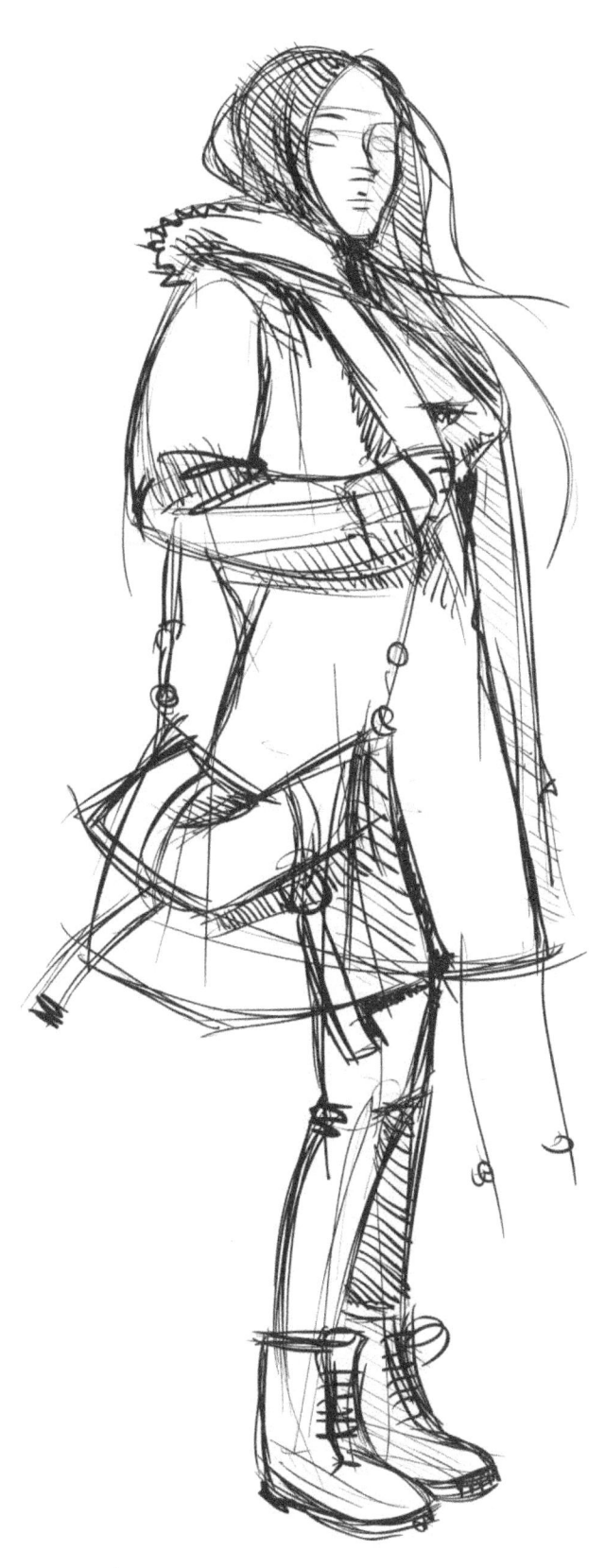

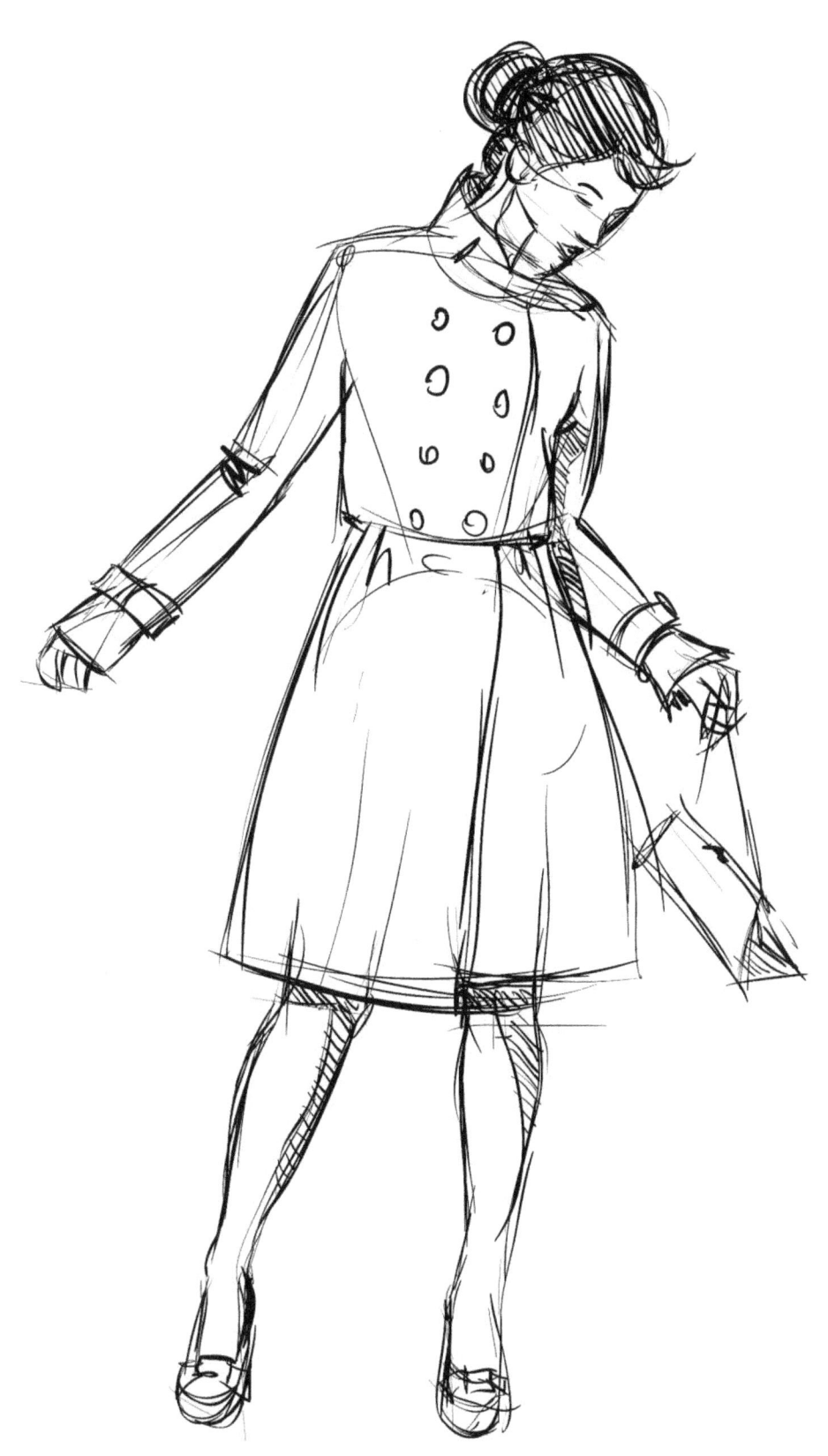

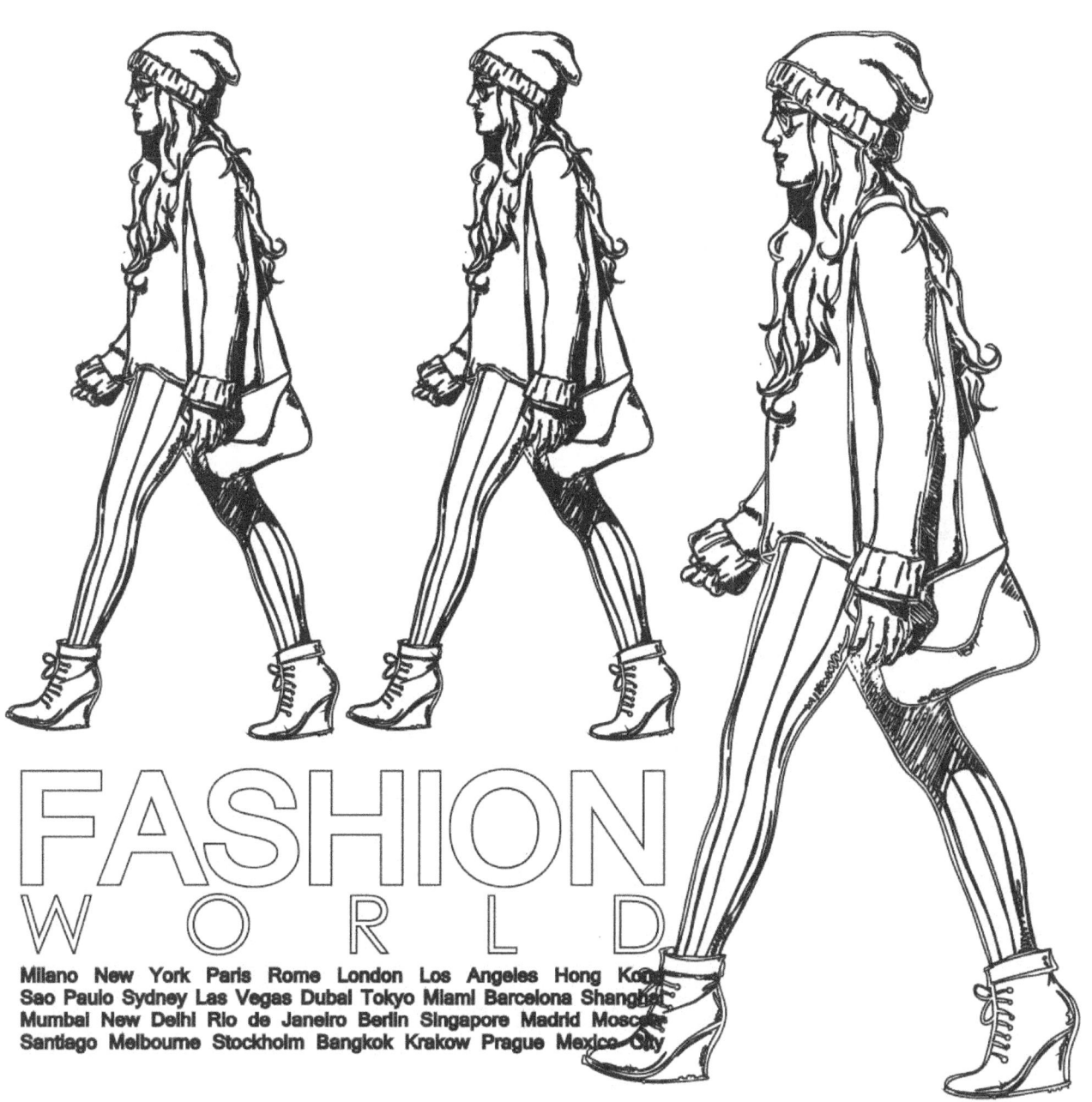

FASHION
W O R L D

Milano New York Paris Rome London Los Angeles Hong Kong
Sao Paulo Sydney Las Vegas Dubai Tokyo Miami Barcelona Shanghai
Mumbai New Delhi Rio de Janeiro Berlin Singapore Madrid Moscow
Santiago Melbourne Stockholm Bangkok Krakow Prague Mexico City

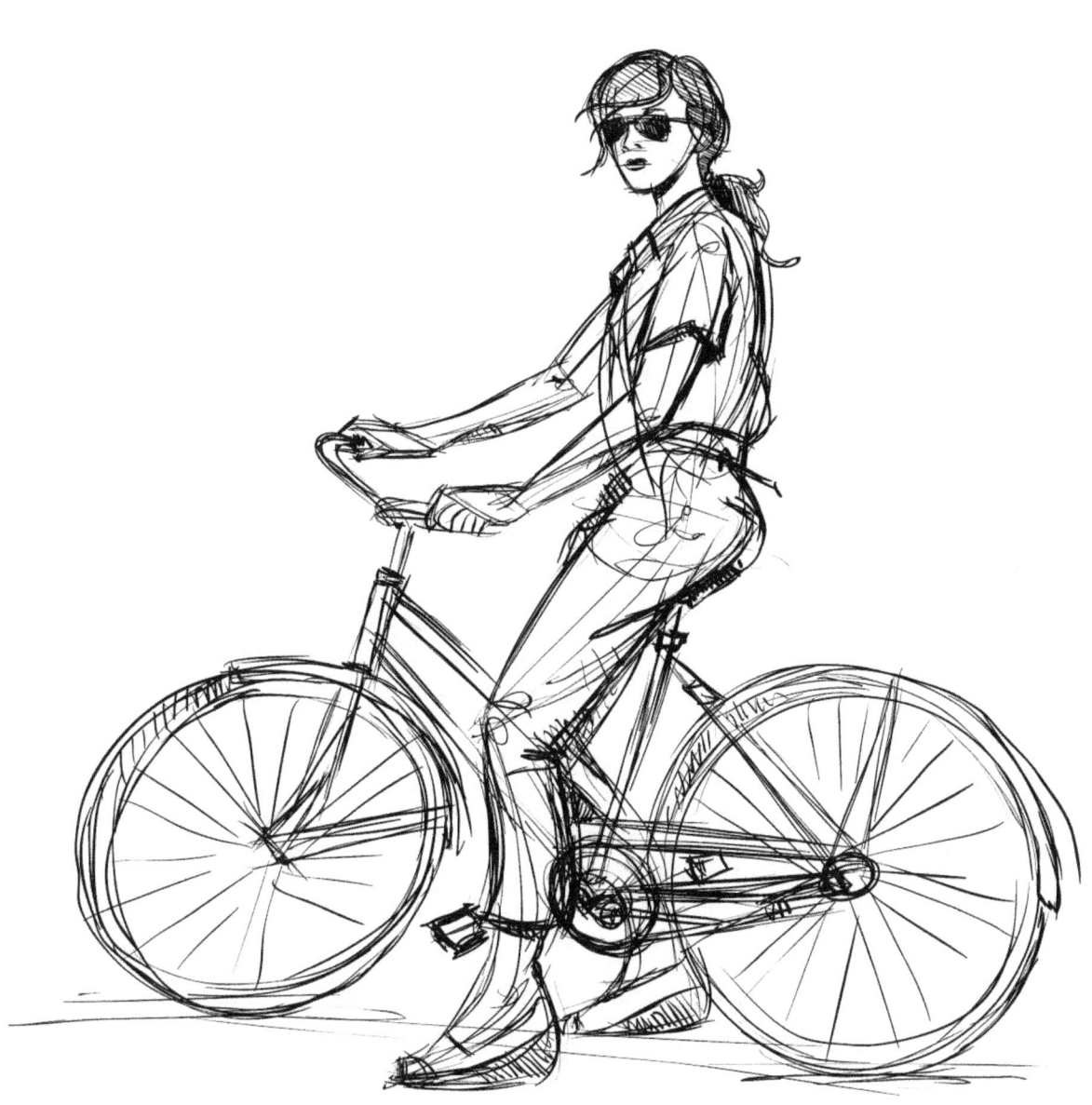

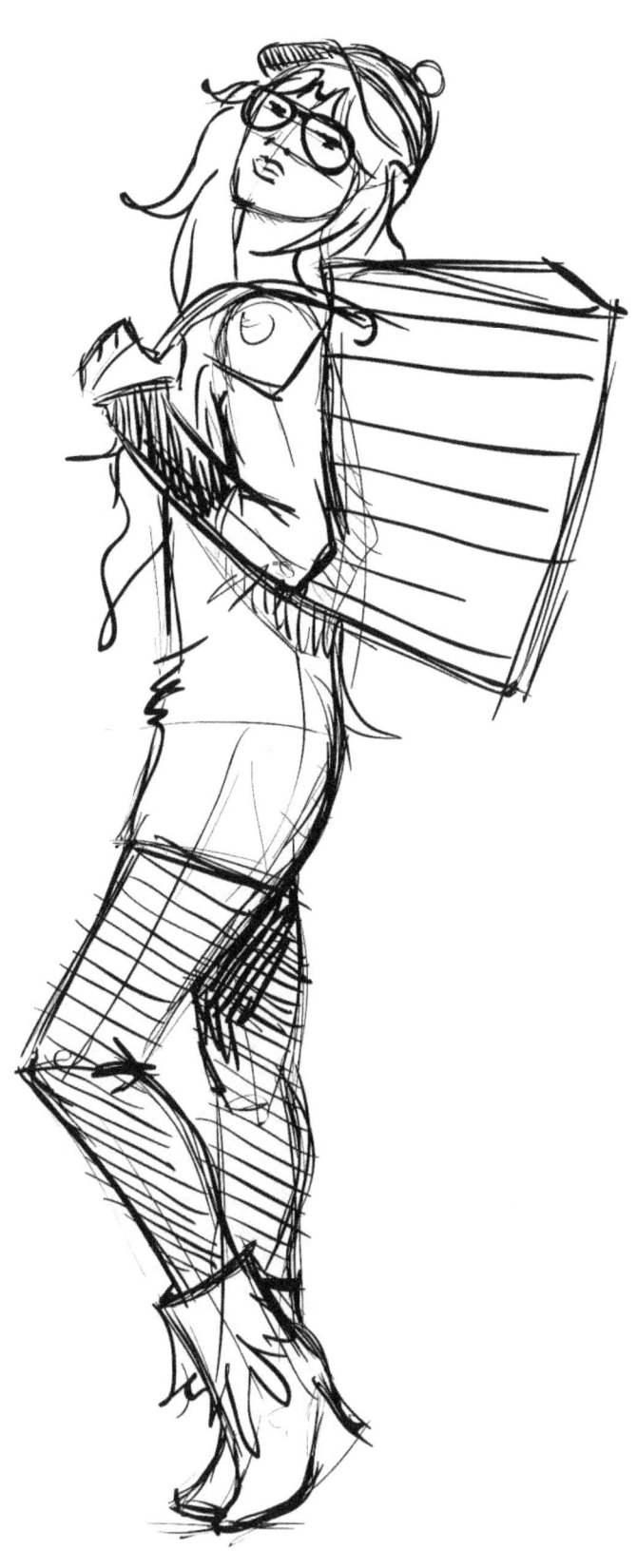

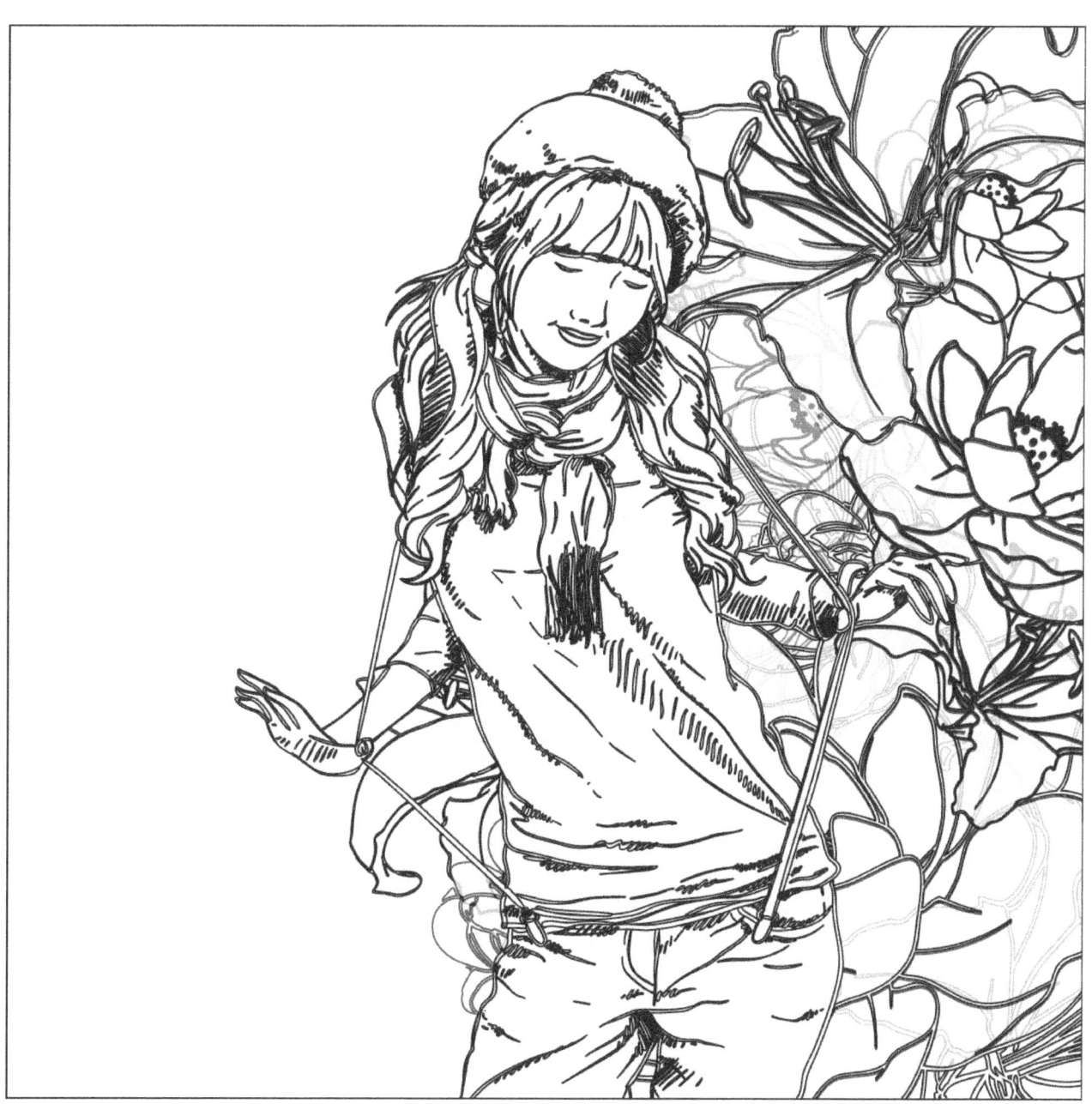

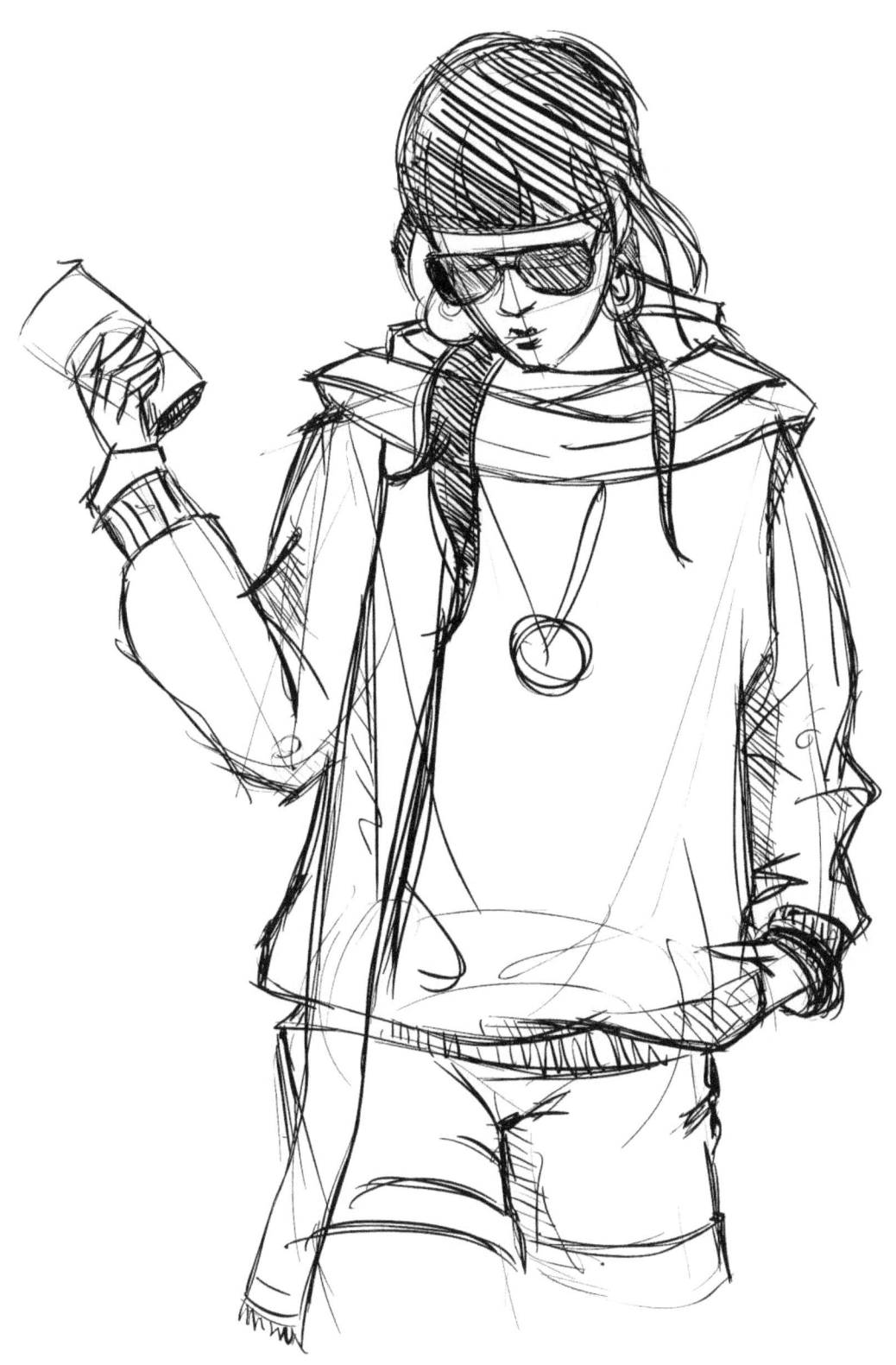

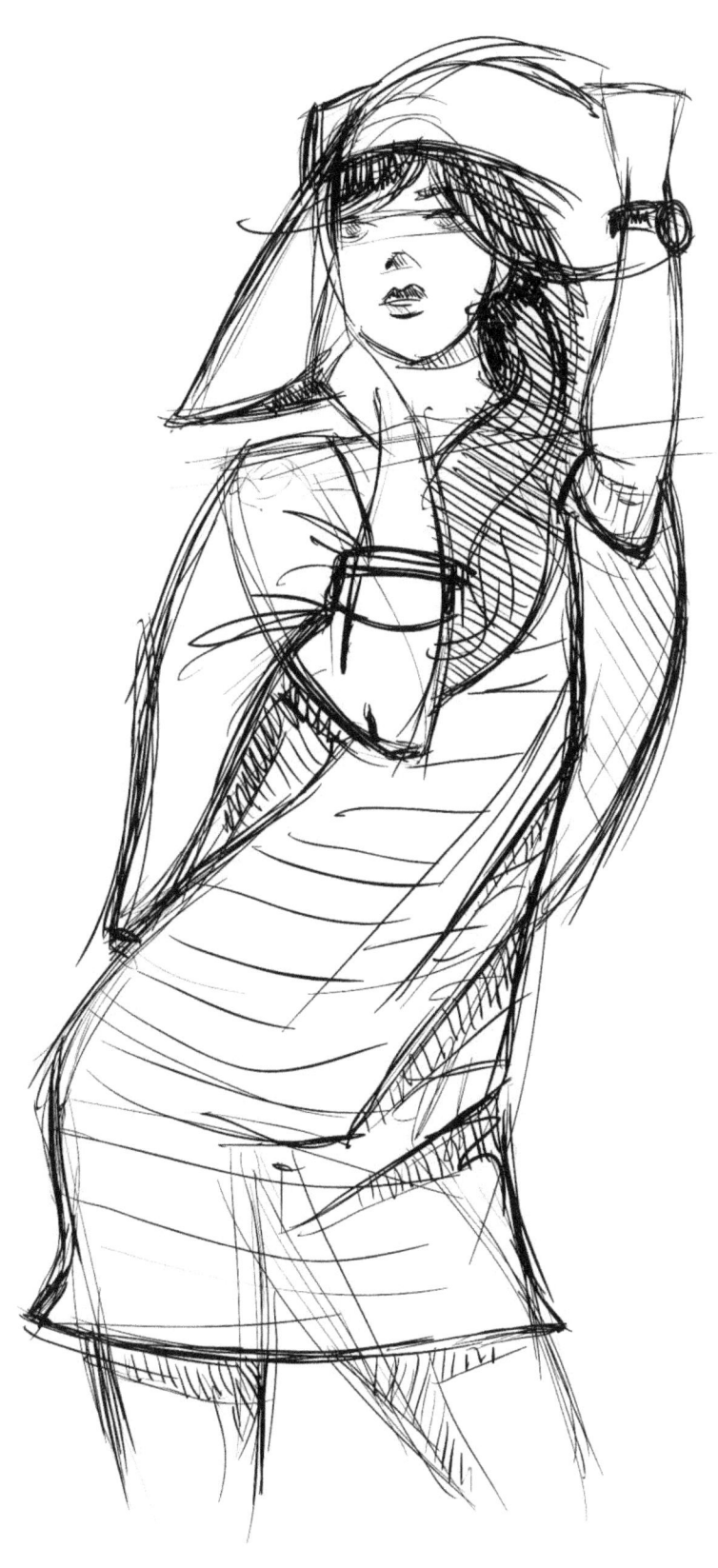

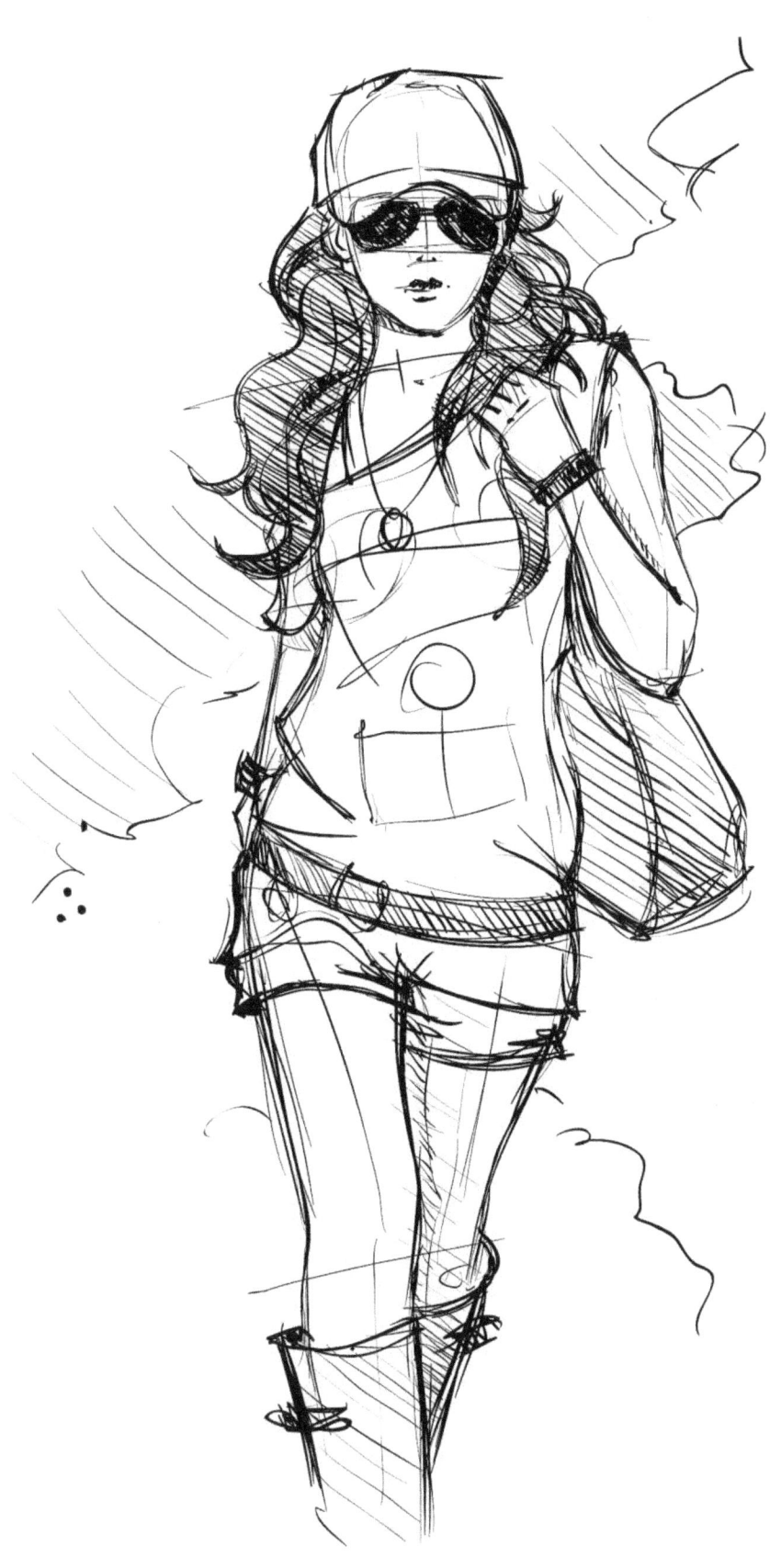

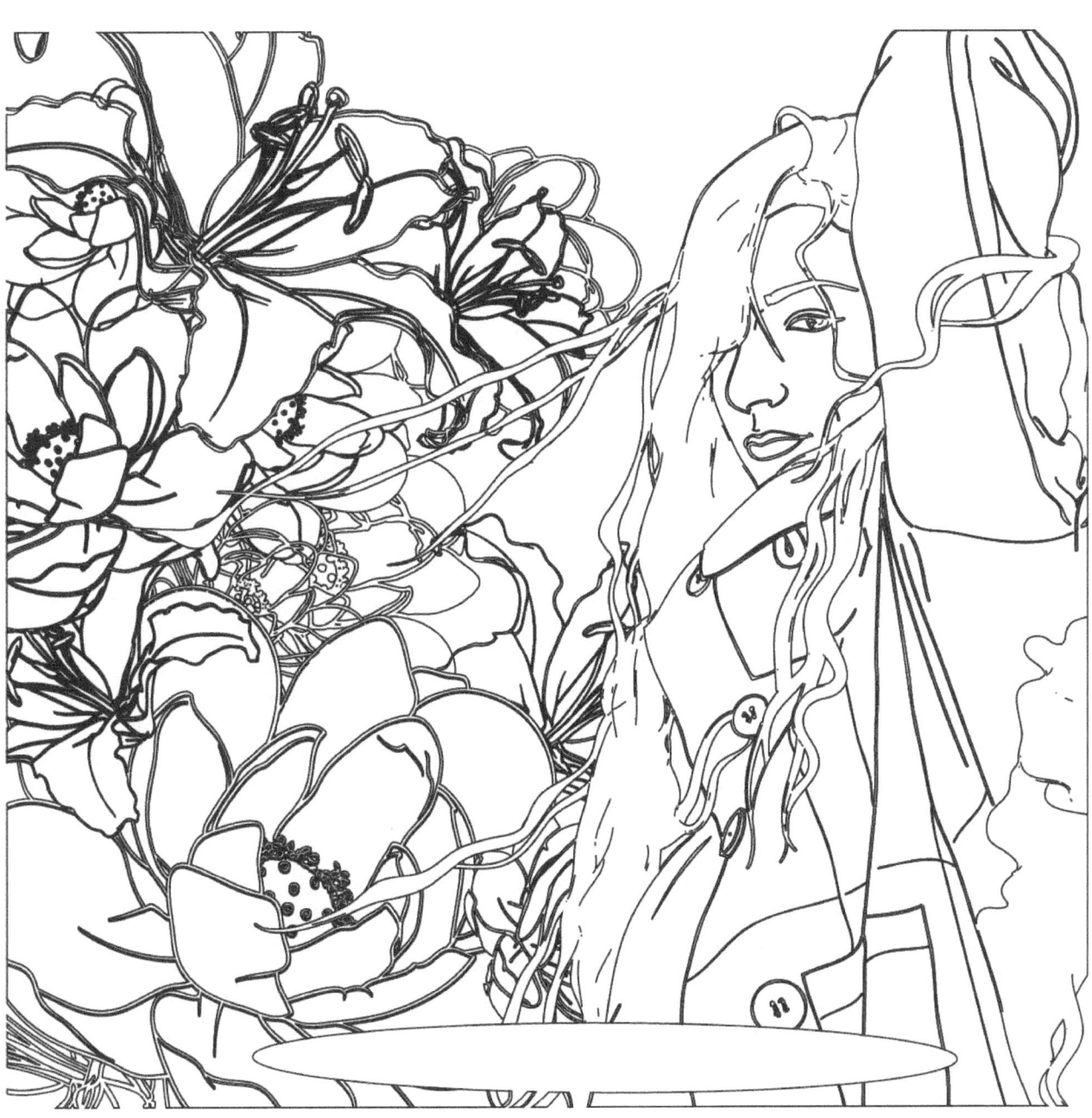

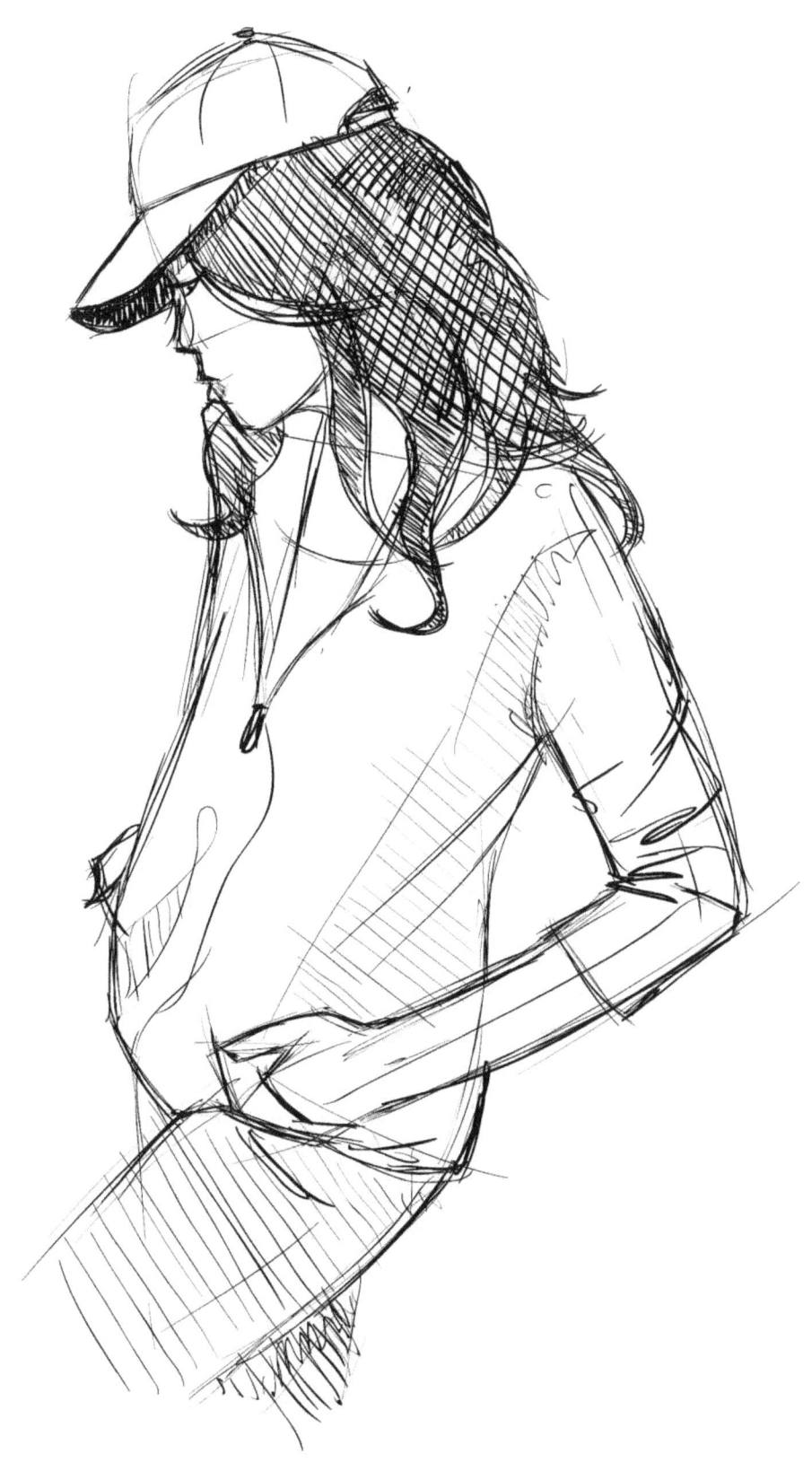

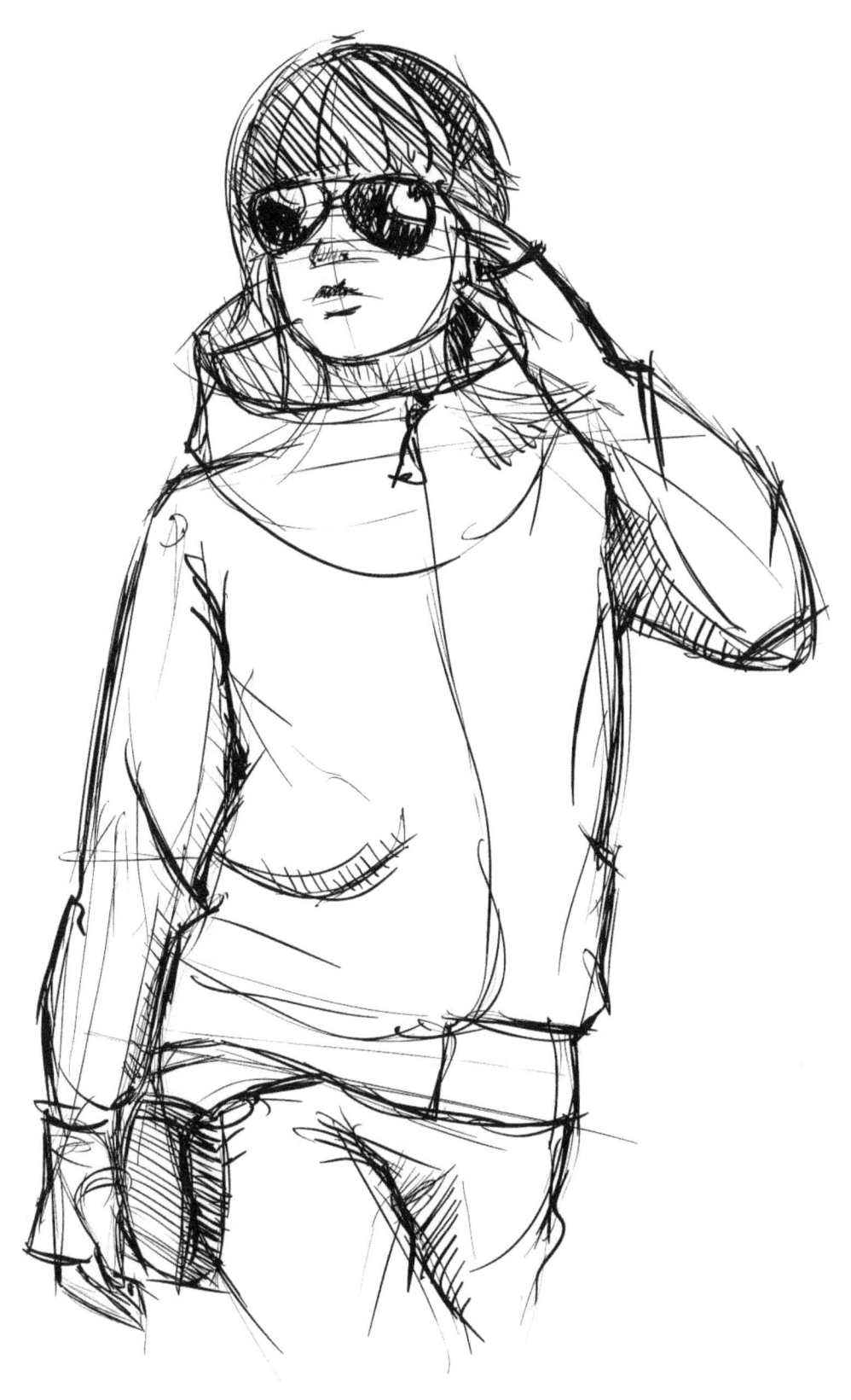

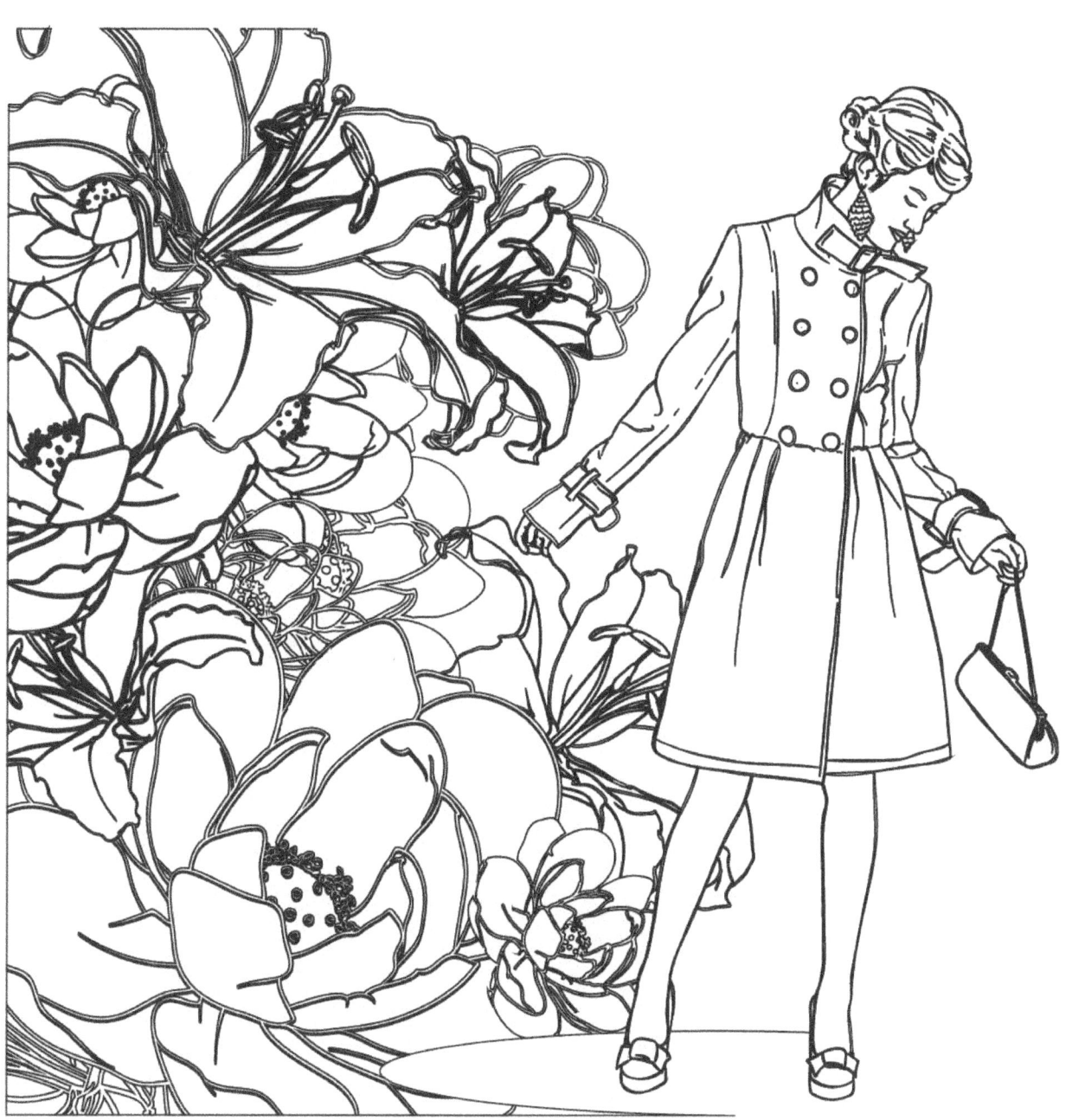

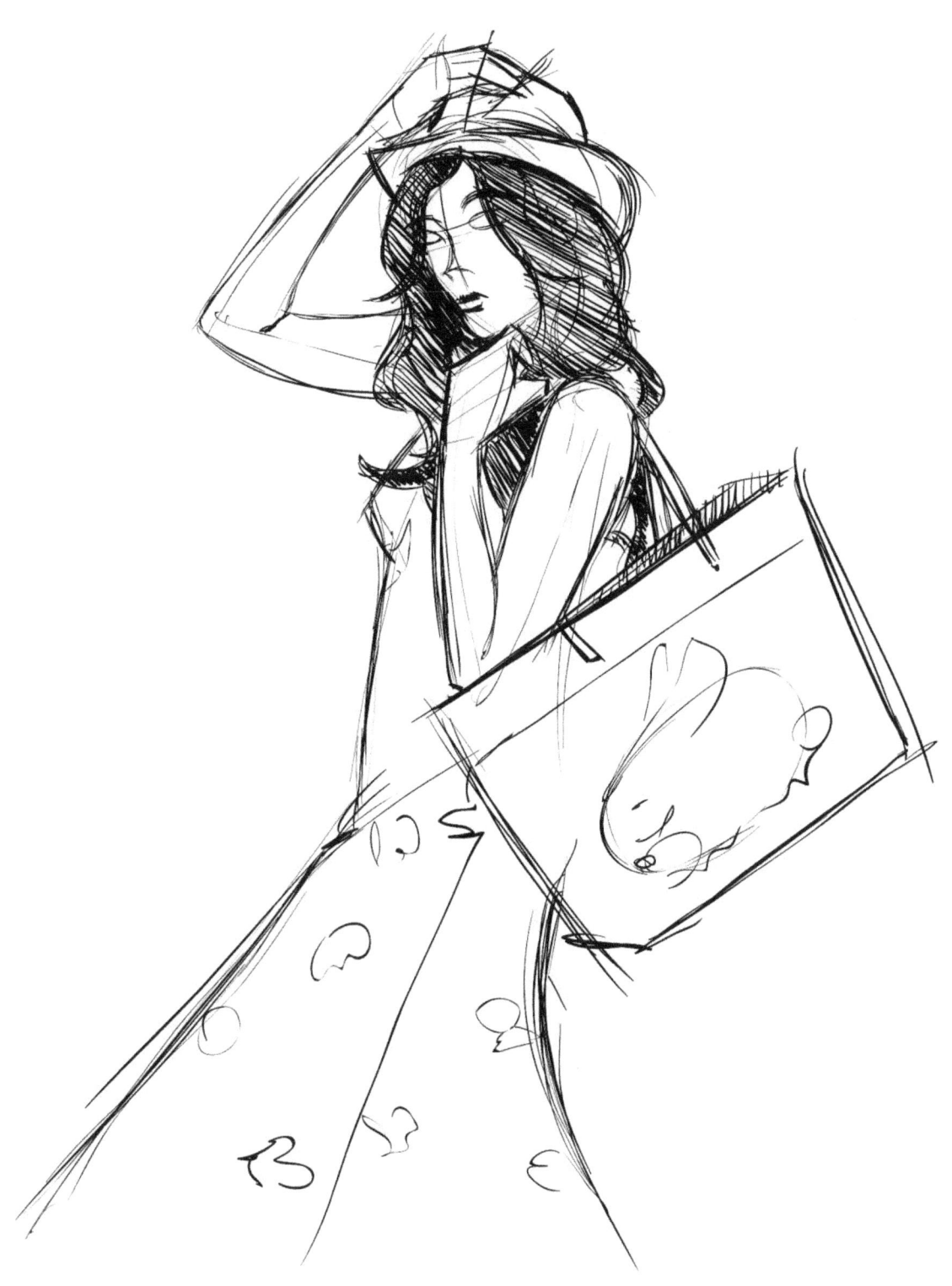

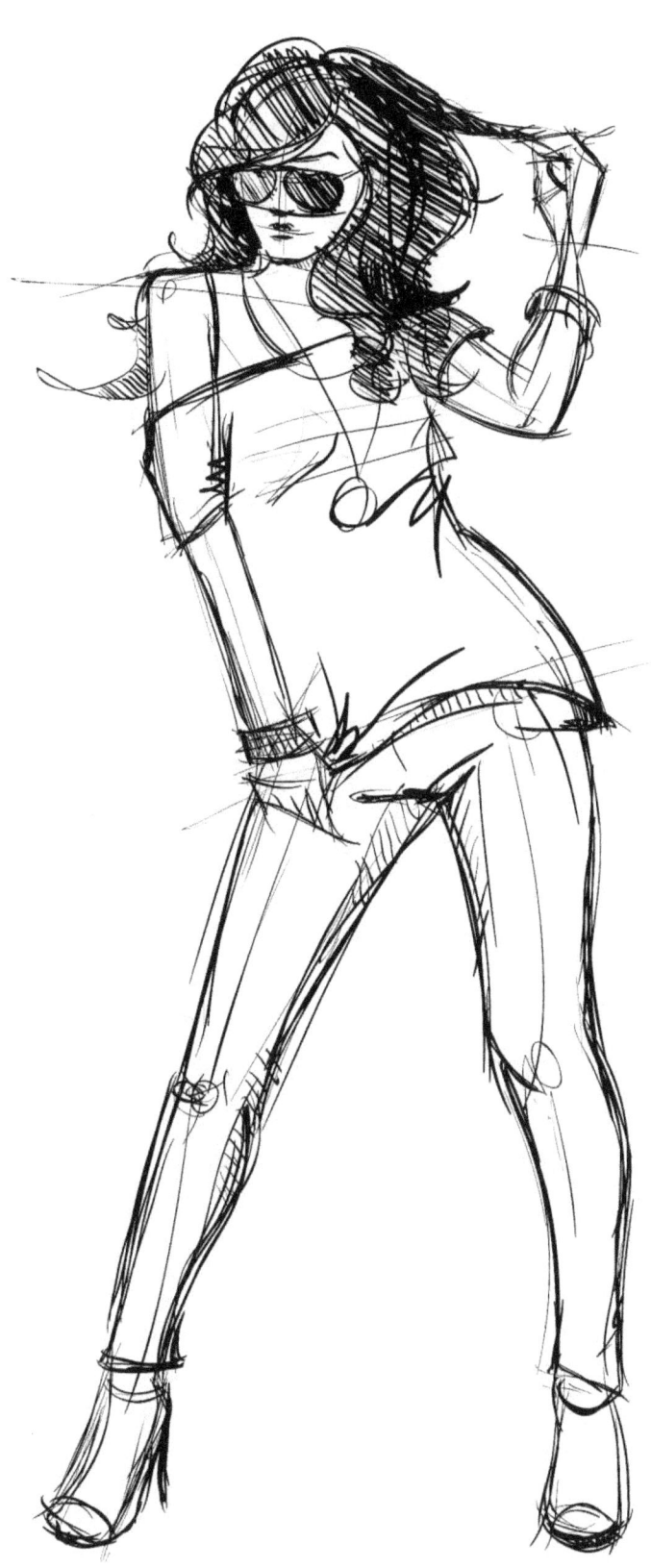

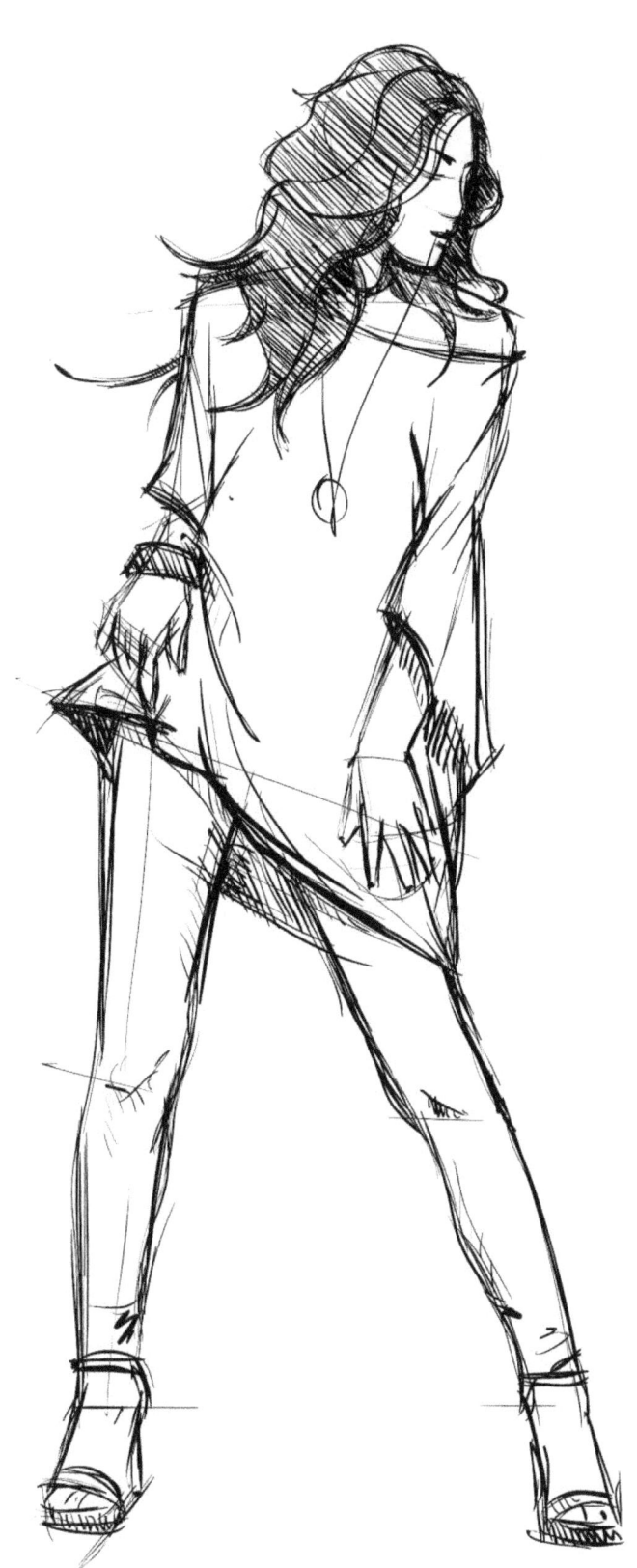